Communities Across America

by Lisa Benjamin

Focus Question: What do people who were born in other countries contribute to communities in the United States? (Students understand how individuals, events, and ideas have changed communities over time.)

Table of Contents

Introduction

The year is 1900. The place is New York City. Crowds of people are on the streets of one busy neighborhood. Some talk to friends. Others shop for food. Young children play ball. Most of the people in this neighborhood are from Italy. With so many Italians living there, it's no wonder it is called "Little Italy."

In the past, many Italians moved to a neighborhood in New York City called Little Italy.

A community is made up of all the people who live in it.

At the turn of the century, many people in the United States were immigrants. They came from Russia, China, and Mexico. They left their homes in Ireland, Scotland, and Germany. They wanted to live in America. After they arrived, they settled in communities across the country.

A community is a group of people who live in the same place. A community can be the size of a town. Or it can be as small as a few streets in a large city. The people of a community share a culture or way of life. Let's take a look at how immigrants contributed to communities across America.

Chapter 1
Arriving in the East

Immigration to the United States was a way to start a new life. Some immigrants wanted to find jobs. Others wanted to go to school. Many wanted the freedom to follow their religion. Leaving their homes to move to America was not easy for immigrants. But it was worth it.

Many immigrants arrived in the eastern part of the continent. They traveled across the Atlantic Ocean from Europe to New York City. Starting in 1892, Ellis Island was their first stop when they arrived. Ellis Island was an immigration station for newcomers.

Immigrants arrived at Ellis Island in New York.

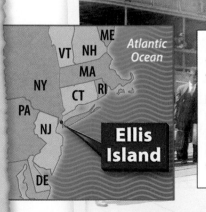

Atlantic Ocean

ME
VT NH
MA
NY
CT RI
PA
NJ
Ellis Island
DE

Discuss: It was difficult for immigrants to leave their homes to come to America. What kinds of things made living in a new place far from home difficult? (Possible response: Friends and relatives were left behind. This would make immigrants feel lonely. Places in the new neighborhood would look unfamiliar and confusing.)

The Wurstfest festival is held every year in New Braunfels.

Once they left Ellis Island, immigrants moved on. Some joined other communities. Some built new communities. Others moved to places where people from their countries already lived. For them, these were a "home away from home."

Many arrivals from Italy and Eastern Europe stayed in New York. Swedish immigrants went to Minnesota. Germans went to Texas. In fact, the city of New Braunfels was established, or started, by German immigrants. They built homes, set up farms, and opened shops. Today, the city holds a festival called Wurstfest to celebrate the culture and **traditions** of Germany.

This photograph shows Fisherman's Wharf in Boston in the 1800s.

During the 1800s, many people from Ireland moved to Boston. In 1847 alone, more than 13,000 Irish immigrants came to that city. Life was not easy in their new home. Many of them were poor. In those days it was hard for Irish immigrants to find jobs. Many people did not want to hire them. Still, Irish immigrants kept moving to America.

Over time, things began to change. The newly arrived immigrants became part of the community. It was easier for them to get work. An Irish person was even elected mayor.

Today, many Irish Americans live in Boston. They still follow some of the old **customs** like cooking Irish food. They take part in a big celebration for the Irish holiday, St. Patrick's Day.

Mary Harris Jones

Newcomers to America have changed the communities they live in. Mary Harris Jones was an immigrant from Ireland in the 1800s. She saw some of the struggles workers faced. Many worked long hours with little pay. Some children had jobs, too. They worked instead of going to school. Mary thought that should change. So, she traveled around the country to fight for the rights of workers. She pleaded for shorter hours and better pay. Her nickname was "Mother" Jones.

Content Vocabulary: **Customs** are the special ways a group of people does something. Customs can include the kinds of meals you make or the music you play. They can also include the ways you celebrate holidays year after year.

Chapter 2

Arriving in the West

Immigration was happening on the other side of the continent too. Immigrants arrived in the west. Many journeyed from Asia to San Francisco.

At first, most of the new immigrants were from China. By 1851, thousands of Chinese immigrants lived and worked in America. In 1910, the city opened an immigration station at Angel Island. Many more Chinese entered America through Angel Island.

Angel Island was often the first stop for immigrants in San Francisco.

Discuss: Ellis Island and Angel Island are two immigration stations that were welcoming immigrants in the 1900s. Today, both places are museums. Why do you think people might want to visit them? (Responses will vary. Students might respond that people visit them to learn about the history of immigration in the United States.)

OR

Pacific Ocean

California

NV

Angel Island

Visitors to Chinatown in San Francisco can buy goods and eat at restaurants.

Chinese immigrants helped build railroads. They also dug for gold. These jobs were difficult and dangerous. But it was hard to find other kinds of work. Over the years conditions changed and immigrants from China became part of the larger community in the west.

Immigrants to the west settled in cities like Los Angeles and Portland. In San Francisco, Chinese newcomers established a new neighborhood called Chinatown. People who lived there could shop in stores operated by other Chinese immigrants. They could eat in Chinese restaurants. Today, Chinatown is still a thriving community.

Other immigrants came from Mexico, Australia, and Japan. They joined communities along the western coast of the United States.

Newcomers from Japan often worked on farms in California. Soon, many Japanese immigrants started their own farms.

Others settled in Seattle, Washington. The **population** of that city grew as more newcomers arrived. By 1930, more than 8,000 Japanese people lived in Seattle.

In autumn, the Japanese Garden in Washington Park is red and green.

Content Vocabulary: Population is the number of people who live in an area. Cities have big populations because many people live and work there. Towns have smaller populations. Populations don't stay the same. They often change. Why might it be important to know the exact population of a city or town? (Possible response: The amount of money put aside for services such as police, schools, libraries depends on the number of people who will need the services.)

Today, many Japanese Americans live in Seattle. You can see how immigrants have helped shape the city. For instance, Washington Park in Seattle has a traditional Japanese garden that was created by a famous Japanese artist. The garden is one of the many reasons why the people of this community are proud to call it home.

Yone Noguchi

Yone Noguchi was one of the first Japanese immigrants to publish poetry in English. He came to America in 1893 and settled in San Francisco. His first English poems were published in 1896. Yone wrote many more poems. Some were in English, while others were in Japanese.

Chapter 3
Communities Today

Immigrants still move to America. They come from all over the world. And they join communities in every part of the United States.

People from Lebanon have settled in Dearborn, Michigan. Many Vietnamese people now live in the city of Houston. There is an Iranian community in Los Angeles. Immigrants from the Dominican Republic have joined the community of Sleepy Hollow, New York.

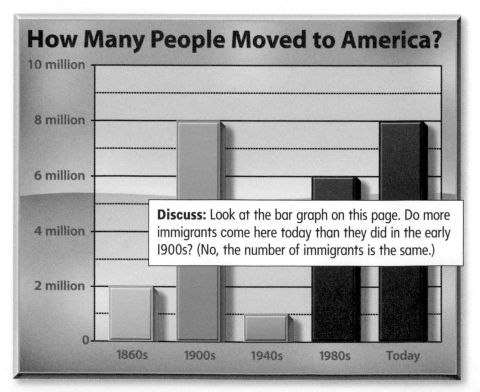

How Many People Moved to America?

Discuss: Look at the bar graph on this page. Do more immigrants come here today than they did in the early 1900s? (No, the number of immigrants is the same.)

Discuss: Imagine a community with immigrants from many different countries. What might it be like? (Students should describe a community that has a variety of people with different foods, celebrations, languages.)

Members of communities share traditions at parties and festivals.

As immigrants join new communities, they bring change. The newcomers contribute their own traditions to their new homes. They celebrate their special holidays. They cook their traditional meals. They share their music, their art, and their stories. Soon these traditions become part of the community.

Today many Mexicans have moved to New Braunfels to work on farms. Now, that city not only has a German heritage, it has a Mexican one, too. Downtown, you can find German restaurants right next to Mexican ones.

Immigrants change communities. But that is not all that happens. Newcomers also take on the traditions of the places where they live. Their children go to school in their new communities. They join the celebrations, play the music, and eat the food of the place they now call home.

They are more than just a group of people who live in the same place!

Glossary

customs *(KUHS tuhmz)* the special ways a group of people does something *(page 7)*

immigration *(i muh GRAY shuhn)* the movement of people from one country to a new one to live *(page 4)*

population *(pop yuh LAY shun)* the number of people who live in an area *(page 10)*

traditions *(truh DISH uhnz)* the practices, or ways a family or larger group does things, that are passed down over many years *(page 5)*

Index

Comprehension Check

Summarize

Use the chart to record details and a main idea about communities in America. Then use the information to write a summary of this book.

Detail
Detail
Detail
Main Idea

Think and Compare

1. Reread page 12. Which sentence states the main idea? What are two details that support the main idea? *(Main Idea and Details)*

2. Which community would you like to visit? Why? Which details in the book helped you answer the question? *(Analyze)*

3. How did immigrants help the United States change and grow? *(Evaluate)*

Sample answers are given:
I. The sentence that states the main idea is "And they join communities in every part of the United States." Students should list two immigrant groups and the places where they settled, such as Vietnamese immigrants who live in Houston.
2. Answers will vary. For example, students might like to visit New Braunfels to attend Wurstfest and learn more about German culture.
3. Immigrants increased the populations of the communities where they settled across the United States. They also brought their traditions, which added to the culture of their new country.